GW00758819

Next Time You See a CLOUD

BY EMILY MORGAN

NSTA **Kids**
National Science Teachers Association
Arlington, Virginia

National Science Teachers Association

Claire Reinburg, Director
Wendy Rubin, Managing Editor
Rachel Ledbetter, Associate Editor
Amanda Van Beuren, Associate Editor
Donna Yudkin, Book Acquisitions Coordinator

ART AND DESIGN
Will Thomas Jr., Director

PRINTING AND PRODUCTION
Catherine Lorrain, Director

NATIONAL SCIENCE TEACHERS ASSOCIATION
David L. Evans, Executive Director
David Beacom, Publisher

1840 Wilson Blvd., Arlington, VA 22201
www.nsta.org/store
For customer service inquiries, please call 800-277-5300.

Lexile® measure: 980L

Copyright © 2016 by the National Science Teachers Association.
All rights reserved. Printed in the United States of America.
20 19 18 17   5 4 3 2

Special thanks to Jack Creilson, meteorologist at the American Meteorological Society, for reviewing this manuscript and answering my many cloud questions.

NSTA is committed to publishing material that promotes the best in inquiry-based science education. However, conditions of actual use may vary, and the safety procedures and practices described in this book are intended to serve only as a guide. Additional precautionary measures may be required. NSTA and the authors do not warrant or represent that the procedures and practices in this book meet any safety code or standard of federal, state, or local regulations. NSTA and the authors disclaim any liability for personal injury or damage to property arising out of or relating to the use of this book, including any of the recommendations, instructions, or materials contained therein.

PERMISSIONS
Book purchasers may photocopy, print, or e-mail up to five copies of an NSTA book chapter for personal use only; this does not include display or promotional use. Elementary, middle, and high school teachers may reproduce forms, sample documents, and single NSTA book chapters needed for classroom or noncommercial, professional-development use only. E-book buyers may download files to multiple personal devices but are prohibited from posting the files to third-party servers or websites, or from passing files to non-buyers. For additional permission to photocopy or use material electronically from this NSTA Press book, please contact the Copyright Clearance Center (CCC) (*www.copyright.com*; 978-750-8400). Please access *www.nsta.org/permissions* for further information about NSTA's rights and permissions policies.

Library of Congress Cataloging-in-Publication Data

Names: Morgan, Emily, author.
Title: Next time you see a cloud / by Emily Morgan.
Other titles: Next time you see.
Description: Arlington, VA : NSTA Kids, [2016] | Series: Next time you see |
    Audience: K to Grade 3.
Identifiers: LCCN 2016027979 (print) | LCCN 2016031754 (ebook) | ISBN
    9781938946363 (print (pbk.)) | ISBN 9781941316320 (print (hardcover)) |
    ISBN 9781941316399 (e-book) | ISBN 9781941316399 (pdf)
Subjects: LCSH: Clouds--Juvenile literature. | Precipitation
    (Meteorology)--Juvenile literature.
Classification: LCC QC921.35 .M67 2017 (print) | LCC QC921.35 (ebook) | DDC
    551.57/6--dc23
LC record available at https://lccn.loc.gov/2016027979

To my friend Kay McLeod, a fellow cloud-watcher and lover of Earth and sky.

"*If there is magic on this planet,*
it is contained in water."
— *Loren Eiseley,* The Immense Journey

A NOTE TO PARENTS AND TEACHERS

The books in this series are intended to be read with a child *after* she has had some experience with the featured objects or phenomena. For example, go outside on a day when you can see white clouds against the blue sky. Lie down on the ground together and observe the clouds. Notice their different shapes and sizes and the directions in which they move. Use your imagination to see different forms. Talk about what you observe and share what you wonder. *Why are clouds white? Why do they float? Where and when did these clouds form? How far have they traveled across the sky to be where you can see them? Where will they go next? Why do clouds appear, change shape, and sometimes vanish?*

Then, after you have had some experiences observing these fascinating phenomena, read this book together. Take time to pause and share your learnings and wonderings with each other. You will find that new learnings often lead to more questions.

The *Next Time You See* books are not meant to present facts to be memorized. They are written to inspire a sense of wonder about ordinary objects or phenomena and foster a desire to learn more about the natural world. Children are naturally fascinated by the ever-changing clouds, but when they realize that clouds are clusters of liquid water droplets and ice crystals floating above their heads, they find the clouds even more remarkable. My wish is that after reading this book, you and your child feel a sense of wonder the next time you see a cloud.

—Emily Morgan

Next time you see a cloud, take some time to stop and watch it for a while.
Does it stay in one place, or does it move across the sky?
Does the shape of the cloud remind you of anything?
Is the cloud changing—growing, shrinking, stretching, or spreading?
How does it compare to the other clouds you have seen?

We see clouds every day and often do not give them much thought. But if you get in the habit of stopping to observe the sky, you might find that the ever-changing display of clouds is one of the most fascinating shows on Earth.
Have you ever wondered what clouds are made of?

Water! Clouds are made of water droplets and ice crystals that attach to tiny particles in the air.

When we look at Earth from space, we can see that our planet is a water planet. We see greenish-brown areas of land, but most of our beautiful world is blue and white. There are blue oceans of water and white ice caps of water—covered in swirls of white clouds of water. Have you ever wondered how clouds form?

When the Sun heats water on Earth's surface, the liquid water *evaporates* and becomes an invisible gas called *water vapor*. When water vapor rises into the cooler parts of the atmosphere, something marvelous happens. The vapor *condenses*, which means it turns back into drops of liquid water. These droplets of water cling to particles in the air—and to each other—to form a cloud. Isn't it astonishing to think that clusters of liquid water droplets can float around in the air above you?

Have you ever noticed that when you breathe out on a cold day, your breath instantly becomes visible? That's because the invisible water vapor in your warm breath quickly cools and condenses into tiny liquid water droplets—your very own cloud!

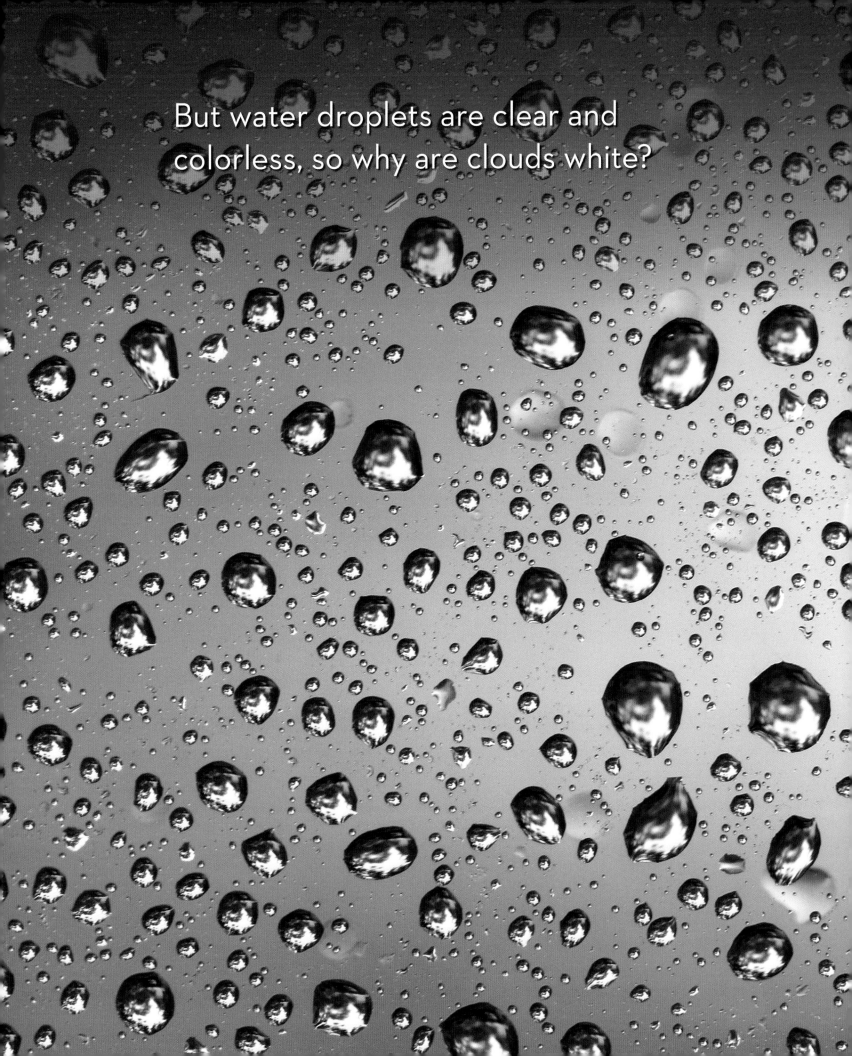

But water droplets are clear and colorless, so why are clouds white?

Clouds are white for the same reason that snow is white. When liquid water droplets or ice crystals are bunched together, they reflect and scatter the light that hits them. They do not scatter one wavelength (or color) of light more than any other. All of the colors of light are scattered equally and combine to make white. Every once in a while, you can see the white light separated into different colors—creating a rainbow—but most of the time the reflected light is white.

As you watch the sky from day to day, you will quickly realize that there are many types of clouds. They can be small, large, thick, thin, high, low, and all kinds of shapes. But scientists recognize three main categories—cirrus, stratus, and cumulus—and each one has many variations.

Cirrus clouds are feathery-looking. They appear as wisps of white high in the sky and are made of ice crystals.

Stratus clouds are sheets of clouds that cover a large area. Blankets of stratus clouds can block some of the sunshine from reaching your eyes, making the clouds look gray. Stratus clouds sometimes produce a steady rain or snow.

Cumulus clouds are big and puffy. You usually see these clouds when the weather is nice. But if cumulus clouds begin to grow tall, it could be a sign that the weather is about to change.

As more and more water vapor quickly condenses, a cumulus cloud becomes taller and fuller, rain begins to fall, and a lot of energy is released. These tall cumulus clouds that can produce rain, hail, and lightning are called *cumulonimbus* clouds. These are the fascinating and sometimes frightening clouds we see during a thunderstorm.

As you spend more time observing clouds, you may notice white streaks that crisscross high up in the sky. These are trails of condensation that airplanes leave behind. These human-made clouds are called *contrails*, which is short for *condensation trails*.

If you've ever lifted a bucket of water, you know that water is pretty heavy. Because clouds are made of water, they must be heavy, too. In fact, scientists estimate that the average cumulus cloud weighs about 1.1 million pounds. That's as much as 100 elephants! If clouds are that heavy, why don't they come crashing to the ground?

The weight of a cloud is spread out over a great distance, and the individual water droplets and ice crystals that make up a cloud are so tiny that the warm air rising underneath them can keep them afloat. If you have ever seen particles of dust in a sunbeam, you have seen how even light currents of air can keep small particles suspended.

But as a cloud grows, the droplets become bigger and heavier, and the cloud eventually does fall to the ground—drop by drop—as rain.

Not all clouds produce rain, though. Sometimes the water droplets that make a cloud are warmed by the Sun and evaporate into the sky, making the cloud seem to slowly disappear.

Have you ever looked up at a cloud and wondered what it would be like to be inside it? Do you imagine yourself jumping on it like a trampoline or falling backward onto it like a soft mattress?

Well, if you have ever walked outside on a foggy day, you have been inside a cloud! Fog is a cloud that's on the ground. Far away in the sky, clouds look thick enough to walk on, but clouds are really just tiny water droplets suspended in the air.

Sometimes the shapes of clouds remind us of things. It's fun to use your imagination to see different images in the clouds. What do these clouds remind you of?

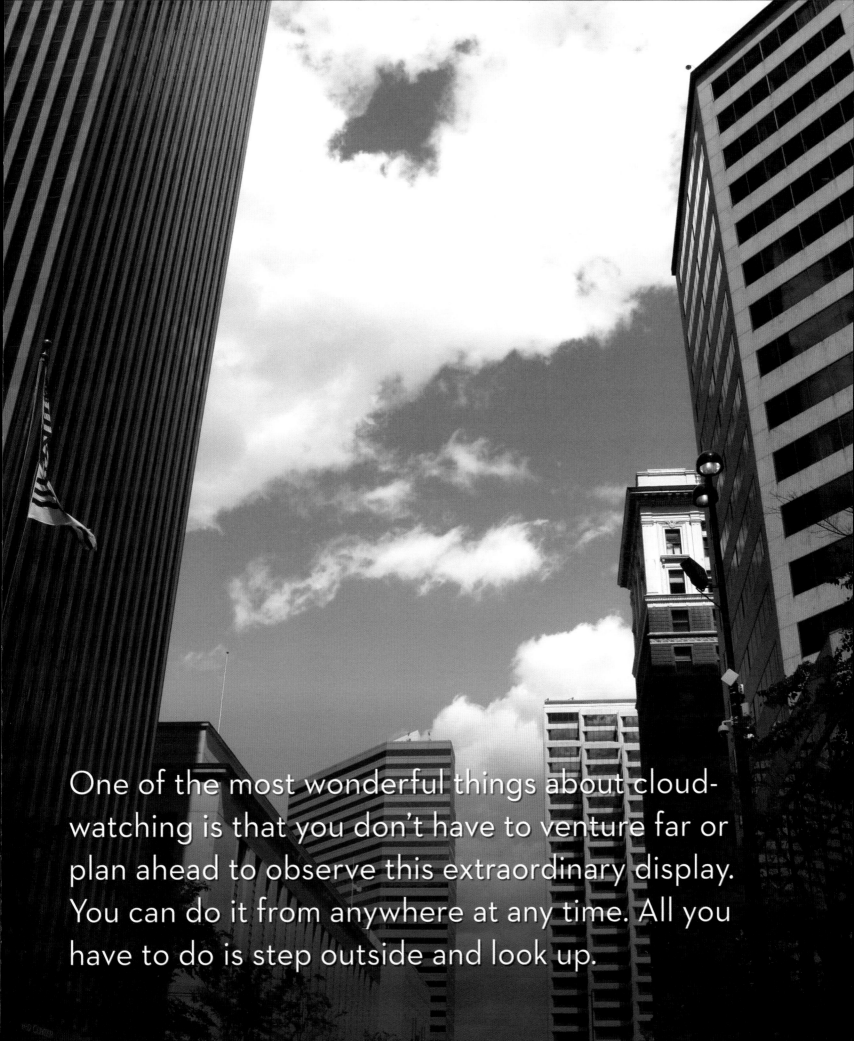

One of the most wonderful things about cloud-watching is that you don't have to venture far or plan ahead to observe this extraordinary display. You can do it from anywhere at any time. All you have to do is step outside and look up.

So, next time you see a cloud, remember that puff of white floating around in the sky is made of water—the same water that fills our oceans, lakes, rivers, and streams. Water becomes invisible as it rises from Earth's surface, then reappears in the cool air above. Water takes the form of droplets and ice crystals clinging together to produce this ever-changing display of infinite shapes and forms. Isn't that remarkable?

ABOUT THE PHOTOS

Clouds reflecting in the water
(Judd Patterson)

Cloud watching
(Tom Uhlman)

Clouds from an airplane window
(Steven David Johnson)

Earth from space
(NASA)

Clouds over a wetland
(Judd Patterson)

Making a cloud
(Tom Uhlman)

Water droplets
(Tom Uhlman)

Cloud and rainbow
(Steven David Johnson)

Cirrus clouds
(Judd Patterson)

Stratus clouds
(Steven David Johnson)

Cumulus clouds
(Judd Patterson)

Rain cloud
(Judd Patterson)

Contrails
(Steven David Johnson)

Lifting a bucket of water
(Tom Uhlman)

Rain cloud
(Tom Uhlman)

Imagining jumping on a cloud
(Tom Uhlman)

Dust in a sunbeam
(Tom Uhlman)

Fog
(Judd Patterson)

Bird cloud
(Judd Patterson)

Flower cloud
(Steven David Johnson)

City clouds
(Tom Uhlman)

Family with clouds
(Tom Uhlman)

Observing the clouds
(Tom Uhlman)

Photographing clouds
(Tom Uhlman)

ACTIVITIES TO ENCOURAGE A SENSE OF WONDER ABOUT CLOUDS

❖ Play the Cloud Shapes game: Go outside with a friend or family member, lay a blanket on the ground, and look up at the sky together. Use your imagination to find different pictures in the clouds. Name the picture you see in the clouds, then challenge your friend or family member to find it.

❖ Take photographs of the sky over several days. Compare the photos and note the similarities and differences between the different clouds.

❖ Download the CloudSpotter app from the Cloud Appreciation Society (see Websites section) to share your cloud photos with experts and cloud-spotters all over the world!

❖ Download the free Sky Watcher Chart from NOAA and NASA (see Websites section). Take the chart outside with you to help you identify the cloud types.

❖ Watch a time-lapse video of clouds forming on the Wonderopolis website (see Websites section).

WEBSITES

Cloud Appreciation Society
https://cloudappreciationsociety.org

NASA S'Cool: Students' Cloud Observations Online
http://scool.larc.nasa.gov

Next Time You See series
www.nexttimeyousee.com

Sky Watcher Chart from NOAA and NASA
www.nws.noaa.gov/om/brochures/cloudchart.pdf

Wonderopolis Wonder of the Day #1413: How Do Clouds Form?
http://wonderopolis.org/wonder/how-do-clouds-form

Downloadable classroom activities can be found at *www.nsta.org/nexttime-cloud*.

REFERENCE

Eiseley, L. 1959. *The immense journey: An imaginative naturalist explores the mysteries of man and nature.* New York: Vintage Books/Random House.